This is Not a COOKBOOK

A Chef's Creative Process from Imagination to Creation

Flynn McGarry

ART BY ADIL DARA

DELACORTE PRESS

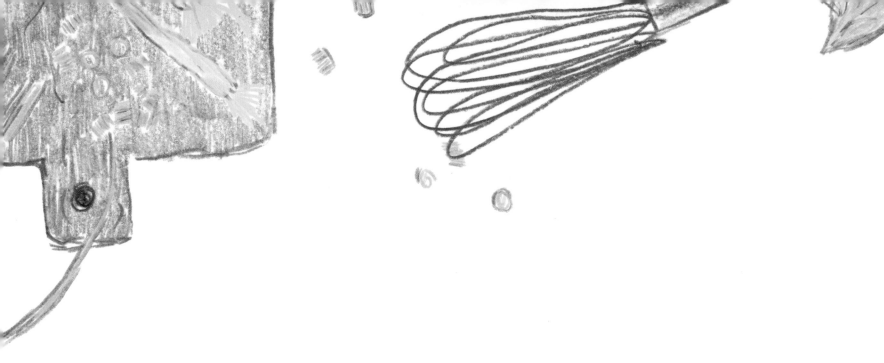

All rights reserved. Published in the United States by Delacorte Press, an imprint of
Random House Children's Books, a division of Penguin Random House LLC, New York.

Delacorte Press is a registered trademark and the colophon is a trademark of Penguin Random House LLC.

Visit us on the Web! rhcbooks.com

Educators and librarians, for a variety of teaching tools, visit us at RHTeachersLibrarians.com

Library of Congress Cataloging-in-Publication Data is available upon request.
ISBN 978-0-593-11969-3 (trade)—ISBN 978-0-593-11970-9 (ebook)

The text of this book is set in 14-point Berling LT Std.

Interior design by Carol Ly and Jade Rector

MANUFACTURED IN ITALY
10 9 8 7 6 5 4 3 2 1
First Edition

This book is for my mom,

who will always be the real writer in the family.

CONTENTS

Introduction

As the title of this book states, this is not a cookbook. You'll find some recipes at the end, but for now, I want to focus on the details of the creative process through food.

The creative process can be confusing, with no clear start or end, so this book doesn't include any "recipes" for creativity. Instead, I've chosen stories from my life that highlight aspects of the creative process, along with decisions that come up along the way. Each story takes you from inspiration to execution of an idea, with some information on cooking peppered in.

Any creative journey will be a long path, but it'll be a worthwhile one. I'm still on mine, always trying to define what's next.

So get creating!

this is not a
bedroom

This Is Not a Bedroom

Most art forms require tools and specialized skills. But even the best tools don't necessarily guarantee you'll end up with the best creations. You could spend thousands of dollars on paints and brushes and still be at a loss as to what to put down on a canvas.

Cooking relies more heavily on tools than most art forms, so it's easy to get caught up in wanting all the gadgets that exist for just about every culinary task. In reality, though, it doesn't take much to be a great cook. As long as you have some basic tools and a vivid imagination, you can create something amazing.

I had many interests growing up. The first that stuck was soccer, but I was convinced I could only be great if I owned the same cleats, shin guards, and uniform as my favorite players. After many trips to the secondhand store, I couldn't find any of the right apparel and soon lost all interest in the sport. Next was baseball, which ended with similar results. I stuck with guitar for a while, even forming a band with friends, but the music we made didn't sound especially inspired.

I left the band when I realized I wasn't going to be as good as John Lennon.

When I was ten I grew tired of my parents' limited cooking repertoire. I wanted to explore different kinds of food and began researching restaurants and cookbooks.

Three restaurants in particular caught my eye and influenced my style.

THE FRENCH LAUNDRY

California's Napa Valley

I got their cookbook as a present for my eleventh birthday. It's filled with hundreds of incredible recipes, and I read it over and over like a page-turning mystery. My biggest takeaways, though, had nothing to do with the food. I learned two equally important things: (1) to use only perfectly cut green tape to label containers, and (2) to have a "sense of urgency" at all times, a phrase that's written beneath a clock in the French Laundry kitchen.

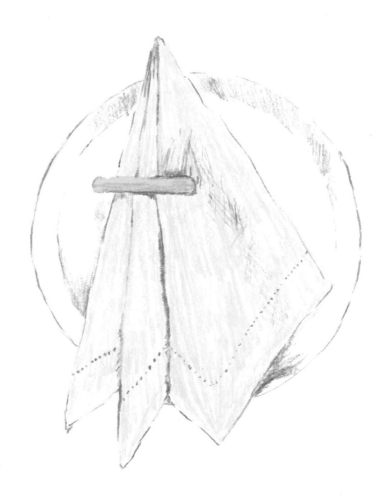

ALINEA

Chicago

Their cookbook opened my eyes to molecular gastronomy, a style of cooking that uses science and new technology to adapt the way food is eaten. The chef, Grant Achatz, had also worked at the French Laundry, which was a dream of mine. The restaurant also made me start obsessing about stainless steel tables.

NOMA

Copenhagen, Denmark

Their cookbook inspired me to learn about wild foods and led to my obsession with Danish Tupperware.

I fixated on emulating these restaurants, down to wanting every piece of equipment and all the resources they had. But with no income of my own, I had to find a way to re-create the dishes of those chefs with what was available to me. What seemed simple turned into an undertaking for my whole family. First, we rearranged our home kitchen so it could function like a commercial kitchen, but my mom wouldn't allow me to get rid of the toaster and coffee maker, so it lacked crucial counter space. The adult counter height also added insult to my not-quite-there-yet growth spurt.

After I deemed our home kitchen a failure, I moved out into the dining room with larger plans. I was determined to cook my way through the French Laundry cookbook and wanted to re-create the brigade-style layout of their kitchen. The brigade system was designed by Auguste Escoffier in the 1900s and has become a classic way to organize a commercial kitchen.

Under the brigade system, the executive chef stands at the "pass," where all the food is finished, and acts as the last check in advance of service. Before a dish even makes it to the chef, it must be checked by the sous-chefs, who are assigned to run different sections of the kitchen. Under the sous-chefs are the chefs de partie, who are each in charge of one station of the kitchen. There is a garde manger station (cold food), a warm appetizer station, a fish station, a meat station, and an entremets (sides of a main course) station. Together, this team of chefs smoothly runs an efficient kitchen where creative energy can be channeled into success.

To achieve a brigade-style kitchen, my dad and I went to a home improvement store and found inexpensive stainless steel counter-tops. We built wood bases for them so they were at the perfect height for me. After arranging the counters in the dining room and moving our dining table into the living room to make space, I had something that resembled a kitchen. My parents let me buy two induction burners, which, along with my collection of pans, turned this arrangement of countertop tables into a functioning kitchen.

THE BRIGADE SYSTEM

EXECUTIVE CHEF

SOUS-CHEF

CHEFS DE PARTIE

Most of the time I was cooking alone and played every role in the brigade. I was literally running in circles and making a mess around my makeshift cooking island.

Putting my kitchen in the dining room created its own challenges. My family would frequently poke and prod my cooking experiments as they passed through the room, and my dog, Digby, always got a little too excited when I dropped something. It was too hectic to create in.

Some people create well in a group setting, but at this point, I realized I wanted my kitchen to be quiet and all-to-myself. I wanted a space where I could create and make mistakes without the pressure of having other people around.

On an especially calm day in the house, I had an idea: the setting for my ideal kitchen was . . . my bedroom! First I measured and drew up how I was going to arrange things. Then I moved each piece of equipment and all my countertop tables into my room. I had a door I could shut and ample windows to ventilate the food smell. Any piece of furniture that wasn't essential got moved out. I folded my twin-sized bed into the closet and tucked away my schoolbooks. The result: my room now resembled a restaurant kitchen rather than the bedroom of a thirteen-year-old, and it immediately made me want to create.

Between moving tables around, I would read my Alinea cookbook. Alinea's food and kitchen were very different from the more traditional French restaurants I had been reading about. The kitchen was much like

its food—it respected the classic style but was open to endless creation. I felt this less rigid approach was closer to what I needed in my bedroom. I arranged the countertop tables to match the layout at Alinea. From the first time I cooked in this reconfigured room, it felt less like a kitchen and more like an open space that was conducive to creativity.

As I began to discover new styles of cooking, the kitchen would continuously morph.

When I was fascinated by grilling, I moved the tables outside, around our old family Weber grill, and created an outdoor kitchen inspired by the one chef Bobby Flay had at his house. With a few cheap metal tables and tireless imagination, I was able to re-create the essence of some of the best kitchens in the world out of my small bedroom.

My parents were used to my room morphing with each new interest, but this latest one was more involved than when I just had

guitars and band posters in my room. They set some ground rules: no open gas flames, and no food left out. Even though I broke their rules a few times, the results of our family dinners outweighed their concerns. They knew how important it was for me to have a space to create and encouraged me to continue.

I was able to re-create many of the dishes of my chef heroes by using what I had on hand. If I lacked a tool or didn't have access to a certain ingredient, I learned to adapt and created my own recipes. That's how I discovered the importance of inspiration in the creative process, as well as the importance of improvisation.

I didn't have to be exactly like my heroes. After all, imitation is not creation. This realization helped me forge my own culinary style.

this is not
weird

This Is Not Weird

Conformity is one of the great enemies of creativity. That's because new ideas are often viewed through a harsh lens, so it's often easier to just conform. Overcoming criticism from others, as well as your own fears, is one of the most important factors in creating something new and unique.

At school, my interests frequently differed from my classmates'.

When I was five, I decided I wanted to dress like my favorite TV character, Bob the Builder. I wore a tool belt every day. Other kids were into skateboarding and video games, but I was afraid of falling and I disliked sitting inside all day, especially with a controller in my hand. So I played with my tool belt, which definitely left me an outlier.

As I grew up, my interests kept drifting further from my peers'. Some of these interests were influenced by my family: I adopted my sister's interest in music, my grandfather's interest in fashion, and my parents' interest in movies. My list of interests kept growing, but I felt I couldn't share them with any of my friends without distancing myself even more.

When my interest in cooking took hold, it immediately outweighed the rest. Initially, I tried to keep it to myself, especially at school, but containing this new passion became impossible. Instead of taking notes in math class, I would draw the dishes that were floating around in my head; art class became more about the fruit we were painting than the still life as a whole; and after-school reading would start with the assigned book and end with a new chef's memoir. At playdates I'd have my few close friends help me in the kitchen. They liked cooking but became easily bored by the painstaking culinary tasks.

Cooking seemed to be something I could relate to, but I got frustrated when my friends didn't take it as seriously as I did. At school, I still felt the need to hide just how much I cared about cooking. My classmates already teased me for my odd interests, not to mention my outfits (inspired by my eighty-year-old grandfather—I didn't exactly fit in with my peers), and I didn't want something that had become so special to me to be fair game for school bullies.

I found solace in cooking at home, reading cookbooks, and watching cooking videos on the internet.

Eventually, I stopped thriving at school. My grades were starting to decline, and my mom saw how unhappy I was. She thought that switching me to another school was the answer. After one day at the new school, we both realized that it wasn't the solution; my unhappiness was bigger than just an individual school. I wanted to have the freedom to explore my new passion fully, without the boundaries of a five-day-a-week school schedule. I wanted to be with people who

understood and shared my passion. I wanted to be on a kitchen line as opposed to in a classroom. We agreed that homeschooling seemed to be the only option. My mom was hesitant at first—homeschooling meant giving up a lot of normal school experiences—but my unwavering commitment to and excitement about cooking convinced her. There was only one condition: I had to agree to finish every math homework assignment.

Not long after starting homeschooling for the eighth grade, I began helping out at a neighborhood café owned by a friend of my mom's. My initial jobs were limited to shaping biscuits, cutting vegetables, and watching the line cooks work smoothly through a busy lunch rush. Being in a professional kitchen immediately made me feel at home.

Putting produce away felt more satisfying and familiar than hanging out with friends after school, and making the staff meal was way better than school lunch. For the first time, I felt like I belonged somewhere.

After working a few months at the café, I wanted to move on to a more challenging kitchen that aligned with the styles I was interested in. My mom bought us tickets to a local food festival so I could experience all the different restaurants in Los Angeles we usually couldn't afford to go to.

I read up on all the restaurants that would be participating. On the day of the festival, I was bursting with excitement. It was the first time I was going to taste the kinds of foods I had only read about, and I wasn't going to miss out on the opportunity to try everything each restaurant was offering. After making our rounds, my mother gently nudged me to speak to the chefs whose food I liked the most and was inspired by.

One of the chefs offered me an internship a few days a week once I told him how much I loved his food. I was thrilled and honored and eager to get started.

On my first day, I showed up with my freshly sharpened knives and my child-sized chef coat pressed perfectly. I was nervous to be around such talented cooks working at a high level, but from the moment I walked into the kitchen I felt the energy I had been craving. Cooks were moving with speed and elegance, getting ready for dinner service. The stove top was full of sauces that were reducing, filling the kitchen with the warm aromas of caramelizing meat.

As I stood peeling radishes, I looked around, trying to learn everything I could by watching the other cooks. I took note of how the meat cook lit the grill and how the pastry cook rolled the bread dough. I was impatient to get going in the real action of the kitchen.

A few weeks into my time peeling and putting away vegetables, the kitchen experienced a particularly busy service. Usually I just tried to stay out of the way. But the meat cook was really backed up and asked me to pitch in. I was so excited it was hard to keep my cool. I jumped into the grill station, helping him pull meat off the grill. The excitement and rush of working a real restaurant service was what I had been waiting for.

I got home that night with a couple of burns and reeked of grilled meat. Exhausted, I plopped down on the couch, but I couldn't wait to go in the next day and do it all over again.

Within the walls of the kitchen, I found people cut from the same cloth as me. The cooks I met obsessed over the same little things and shared the same challenges. As I got to know my coworkers, I learned that many of them also felt distant from the rest of the world and considered the kitchen a safe haven. Even though my coworkers were around twice my age, they treated me as one of their own, and eventually became my friends.

I started to appreciate the kitchen as a cultural space as well as a workplace where I could learn from people with years more life experience than me. The kitchen became my comfort zone, a place where nothing mattered besides the task at hand.

I was fortunate to find a community of like-minded people who helped me gain the confidence to pursue my dreams. Working with cooks who were as determined as I was to succeed also pushed me in ways I couldn't have imagined. And while there were some chef peers who called me "weird," I met many more whom I related to and who respected me. I started to realize that I wasn't weird—I just hadn't found a group who understood my passion until now.

this is not a

house

This Is Not a House

It can take years to realize a creative dream. Having goals and plans is a start. An equally important part of the creative process involves experimentation and execution. Experimentation gives you the chance to learn more about what you want out of your dreams; execution gives you the chance to learn how to achieve your dreams. Together, the two will push your creative ideas forward and let you experience parts of your dreams right now.

When I was thirteen years old, I was balancing both my homeschool schedule and a full-time restaurant internship. But I still wanted to find a creative outlet. I was learning so many new skills at work and would daydream about how I would use them in my own restaurant one day. I was far from being able to have a restaurant, but I still wanted to be able to cook my own food. On weekends, I started to integrate my new skills into my home cooking. I would often make too much food for my small family, prompting my mother to invite her friends over for dinner. At the time, I was used to cooking only for myself or a couple of family

members, so having a new crowd of diners excited me.

Cooking for a group sparked a new feeling of satisfaction. I loved watching people enjoy my creations; it made the hard work worthwhile. I convinced my mom to invite her friends over once a month so I could try out my new ideas. I wanted the dinner parties to feel like a real restaurant. In order to make that happen, I had to bring on a team—a team that would let a thirteen-year-old boss them around. Three close friends from my old school, along with their parents, seemed like the best candidates.

These friends would join me after school to help cook for the evening guests, and more often than not, their parents would end up doing the dishes at the end of the night. My friends' help was limited to light prep work, heavily directed by me, but their interest mostly revolved around the free pizza staff meal that we ate before the guests showed up.

For these monthly dinners, my bedroom kitchen would transform into a restaurant-style service kitchen. My workstation/school desk became the "pass," complete with an expediting station, and my mom and sister would step in as servers. I wanted every element of the dinners to feel as close to a true restaurant experience as possible, down to printed-out menus and a coat check.

With each dinner, the guest list grew. It started with just close friends and family and mushroomed to include friends of friends. As word spread and more and more people grew intrigued about the "kid who could cook," we decided we could serve up to sixteen people.

One evening, a family friend brought a writer from the *New Yorker* to dinner. He wrote a small piece on the monthly supper club we ran out of our San Fernando Valley home, detailing the unusual team comprising kids and family. When the article came out, interest in the dinners exploded beyond anything we could have ever expected.

It usually took weeks to prepare for each dinner, with my mom and me handling most of the organizing. We confirmed reservations, tested dishes, paid vendor bills, and rearranged our home to resemble a restaurant dining room. Now we had a one-thousand-person waiting list. It was definitely starting to feel like a real restaurant.

CORN

EMBER ROASTED CUSTARD WITH HAM HOCK, BLACK GARLIC,

CHERRY CONFIT IN BEEF FAT, PISTACHIO, FLOWERS

LIOCO ROSÉ, "INDICA" MENDOCINO COUNTY   CALIFORNIA 2013

BLOOMED WITH

GREEN MUSSEL

GLAZED WITH THAI CURRY, COCONUT, LEMONGRASS, PICKLED DAIKON

SPOT PRAWN

TARTARE WITH AN EMULSION OF ITS HEAD, CAVIAR, CELERY, MEYER LEMON

CHARTOGNE-TAILLET, CUVÉE STE. ANNE   MERFY, FRANCE NV

SNAPPER

CANTALOUPE, PUFFED RICE, SESAME, SHISO

FUKUOKA, JAPAN

We tried to execute everything at a high level with limited funds. Guests would pay a small fee to cover the cost of the ingredients, but all the other expenses, like plates and glasses (of which there were plenty!) and special equipment, fell on us. I was such a frequent customer at the local restaurant supply store, always looking for deals, that everyone knew my name.

When I wanted to create a dish that required equipment we didn't have, I had to learn to adapt. We were operating above our means, but I couldn't buckle under all the new demand. What I had intended to be a way to try new ideas quickly became near full-time jobs for my mom and me. The dinners became a practice run at having my own restaurant, including handling all the difficulties that come with it.

After a full year of these monthly home dinners, they were starting to outgrow our home. I needed more space to create and wanted to be in a restaurant kitchen. Also, an increasing number of strangers were trying to attend the dinners, so my mom agreed that it was time to move them to a public space.

A chef I had met while helping with a collaborative dinner invited me to use his restaurant on the one night they were closed. The restaurant was large: 120 seats, and the kitchen was filled with commercial stoves, dishwashing pits, and combi ovens. I'd always wondered what I would create with access to a professional kitchen, and now I finally had the opportunity.

I was so eager to impress the dinner guests that I pushed myself to create an entirely new and ambitious menu. It consisted of eight courses and used every new and impressive technique I could think of. The dinner sold out almost instantly, filling all 120 seats, a huge jump from the sixteen guests at home. This required a new way of cooking for me. But I was overjoyed that I was going to be in charge of a restaurant the size of the ones I read about and dreamed of visiting.

Chefs who run a restaurant of this size usually have over a decade of experience in the restaurant industry. I had been alive for three years over a decade, but I was determined to succeed. I prepared in every way I knew, reading through all my cookbooks for tips and watching videos of professional kitchens in action.

The day of the dinner finally arrived. I showed up before everyone else, early in the morning, prepared to cook and lead. To help execute my vision, I brought in experienced sous-chefs I had worked with in the past. I knew they were better than I was at running a kitchen and felt more confident having them there. We prepped through the day, using every inch of the large, gleaming kitchen. We used all the new equipment as well: liquid nitrogen, sous vide machines, wood-fired grills, and Pacojets.

LIQUID NITROGEN

SOUS VIDE MACHINE

WOOD-FIRED GRILL

PACOJET

As we went into the dinner service, everyone's nerves started to spike. We were about to serve 120 guests a menu that no one had cooked before.

A dinner service moves fast and is usually over before you realize it. I was running back and forth between stations, making sure the food came out as I wanted it to, but I couldn't be everywhere at once. By the end of the night, the team felt a general sense of accomplishment, but I was sure I had lost control over the food. I had dreamed of cooking for many people and having a large team, but this had been my first shot at it, and I didn't feel the same satisfaction I got from our dinners at home. I realized that

I wasn't ready to continue with events on this scale or to lead teams of that size just yet. I was momentarily disappointed—my dreams outweighed my skills. But at least I knew what I needed to focus on to move forward.

I left that dinner with a wealth of new knowledge and a new perspective on where I was in my career. I now needed to figure out what I was going to do next. We'd accumulated a large fan base for these dinners, and I wanted to keep pushing myself. Only one thing made sense: I shifted my direction and looked for a much smaller restaurant, one with only twenty seats, something more similar to what I was used to at home.

I asked chefs I knew if anyone had a restaurant that would fit my needs. One recommended I talk to the chef of an Austrian restaurant in Beverly Hills. The space was the perfect size, and the restaurant was closed two days a week. The chef was passionate about supporting young cooks and decided to let me do one dinner before committing to a monthly agreement.

With my mom's help and a few chef friends, I arranged my first dinner. The smaller kitchen and dining room felt comfortable and familiar. But I wanted to make the space more personal. We made a wooden sign inscribed with the word *Eureka*, which was the street we lived on, as an homage to our home dinners. We covered the wooden tables with tablecloths, made custom silverware holders and printed menus. By dinnertime the space was transformed. We prepped through the day with ease, having to make only twenty portions of everything as opposed to 120. When we opened the doors to our guests, I felt like I was in my own house.

Even the service felt entirely different from my last, larger dinner. I was able to be on the line, working alongside the other cooks, and at the end of the night, we collectively felt the satisfaction I had been striving for.

We continued to host these dinners every month, and with each dinner I learned new things about my passion and about running a restaurant. The pop-ups also helped forge my artistic style and leadership skills. Between each pop-up, I was able to reflect on the previous dinner and adapt the next to focus on my new ideas.

EUREKA

My dream of running a restaurant was beginning to gel into a reality, but I knew I had a lot more to learn and accomplish before I could achieve it. I kept working under and learning from chefs I admired while doing my pop-ups. The pop-ups taught me valuable lessons and helped me define what I wanted out of my dreams.

Having a dream was always important to me, but I never wanted to wait to start living it. Because I found a way to experiment and have failures early on, I was able to define what I wanted out of my dreams and to identify how I could achieve them.

Whatever the path you take, there is always a way to start finding your own creative voice early on. Achieving your dreams may seem far into the future, but the opportunity to experiment and learn on the way is essential. You'll never know what you want out of your dreams until you start to experience them.

this is not a
beet

This Is Not a Beet

One of the best ways to inspire creativity is to identify your problems, prejudices, and dislikes and use them to create something that brings you joy. Thinking critically is essential if you don't want to settle for the norm. It allows you to look at every problem as one that can be solved, as opposed to one you just have to live with.

My problem was beets. In the mornings before school, my dad would try to serve me a pulpy deep-red glass of beet juice. I found everything about the juice unattractive, from its foamy top to its aggressive parental appeal. I needed to find a way to avoid beets.

My dad would also roast beets for dinner. The roots came out of the oven golden brown and sweet from the slow roasting, but the majority of my portion still went to my dog. I couldn't kick my distaste for the vegetable and found myself avoiding beets in the grocery store and at the dinner table.

Then one day, things changed.

I was growing more confident in my cooking techniques and was spending time learning all the ways to cook vegetables. At work, I had to cook and peel pounds and pounds of beets for a new dish the chef added to the menu. My hands seemed to be permanently stained a deep red from the vegetable. I roasted and peeled these beets daily, each day getting more versed in the ways of the beet.

I still wasn't keen on the taste of the root vegetable. I found it overly sweet and watery. But after weeks of looking at beets, I found parts of them rather beautiful. They come in almost every color imaginable: classic red, bright orange or yellow, white, pink, and even pink-and-white striped!

The beets' raw beauty inspired me to give them another shot. I was usually drawn to ingredients that were exciting-looking, whether they were colorful or interestingly shaped. So the beet seemed like the perfect challenge for my next dish. I just had to get over the fact that I really disliked the taste of them, but I enjoyed thinking of it like an experiment and entered a long journey of beet cookery.

I started by
identifying exactly
what I disliked about
beets—the sweetness, the
texture, and my experiences
of being forced to eat them.

Now that I knew what was wrong,
I needed a plan to solve my beet conundrum.

I began to think about what I wished they could taste like. I thought about their vivid bloodlike color and I wondered if they could ever provide the same satisfaction as a perfect golden-brown juicy and savory piece of steak. But now I had something else to figure out: What makes a steak so delicious?

I opened my cookbooks and computer to start researching. I learned that the caramelization created when browning food is called the Maillard reaction. It creates a depth of flavor and furthers the food's umami—savoriness. I thought I could achieve both of these things with the beet. I just needed to do a bit of experimentation.

To get the texture to resemble a steak, I decided to cook a beet very slowly in the oven, at a low temperature, to draw out most of its liquid. The beet came out shriveled and almost half its original size. I bit

旨味

umami
(oo-maa-mee)

into the unrecognizable root and found the texture perfect, but the flavor was still distinctly beetlike. I tried cooking another one, this time adding smoked beet juice and soy sauce. Smoking food with wood chips can add layers of flavor to any food—it's the reason barbecue tastes so good. I also needed to find a way to add umami to the beet. Soy sauce is one of the most umami-rich ingredients a chef can use and would add the needed saltiness. The combination of these two flavors worked! I took a bite of this new beet and found myself enjoying my vegetable foe.

The beet was still missing something. The balance between meat and fat on a steak is crucial to its flavor, and beets have no fat. I hadn't a clue how to make a beet grow fat. I couldn't feed the beet to fatten it up like you'd feed an animal.

One night, while I was scrolling through Instagram, I came across a particularly appetizing photo of a beef Wellington. I had never made beef Wellington and didn't know much about it. I'd seen Gordon Ramsay make it on a cooking show once—the beef tenderloin wrapped in mushroom paste, prosciutto, and puff pastry sounded delicious. I thought if I wrapped the beet in buttery puff pastry, it would solve the need for fat and still keep the dish vegetarian.

I took my beet and covered it in mushroom paste, then in beet greens instead of prosciutto, and wrapped the whole thing in puff pastry. I put the new creation into the oven and waited anxiously. As I removed it from the oven, it glistened, perfectly golden brown on the outside and oozing red juice.

I enthusiastically devoured the Wellington of beets and loved every bite. It was as satisfying as the most delicious steak. I was starting to fall in love with beets. But the dish wasn't complete yet.

Right now it was just a sliced beet Wellington; it needed some sides. I had been reading a book on traditional French sauces that I'd found at an old bookstore. I had spent a month studying the rigorous steps it takes to make these sauces, while ignoring the rigorous steps of my algebra assignments. I was particularly drawn to the Bordelaise sauce—a sauce traditionally made from meat scraps, meat stock, and red wine, reduced until it's a dark shade of brown. I wondered if I could achieve the same deep flavor and richness of the sauce, along with a bloodred color, using only beets. The complex sauce was the perfect complement to a flaky beet Wellington. After the long process of experimentation, the beet Wellington became my favorite dish to make. It also inspired me to discover what else could be done with vegetables. If I could now love the formerly dreaded beet, what else could I think of?

I started to care more about the way vegetables are grown. Why those grown in healthy soil taste better than those that aren't given enough nutrition. I also started to become more informed about meat eating. I consider our society's relationship with meat unhealthy—most of the United States eats too much of it, and we don't raise livestock in a healthy way. After my research, I decided that the best way to change my approach to cooking—and eating—was to find the beauty and deliciousness of vegetables.

As I focused on vegetables as the star of the show, I found myself craving meat less. There are so many unique vegetables and infinite ways to enjoy them, even if it takes a bit of creativity to make them mouthwatering.

With a little effort, I was able to elevate even my most hated ingredient into something incredibly delicious.

My experience with beets changed the way that I looked at ingredients. I learned to treat not only ingredients I cooked with but also most problems in any creative process like puzzles that need solving. Now every time I come across something that challenges me, I ask myself, "Can I do anything to solve this?"

If we all figure out how to conquer our own biases, what greatness can we create?

this is not a

spoon

This Is Not a Spoon

In many ways, food is related to art and design. All three rely on the same basic principles in the creative process.

These art forms are also influenced by aesthetics. The way you see and experience food can dramatically change the way you enjoy it. Just as observing a work of art in the wrong context can ruin the experience of the piece, experiencing food in the wrong context can make it hard to appreciate what you're eating, and can prevent the dining experience from feeling like a temporary escape from day-to-day life.

Restaurants and homes are filled with nuances that influence your experience and relationship to food. Dinner can be one of the best ways to decompress after a long day, or celebrate a special occasion, or enjoy some time alone, but it's the details that make it special.

My art teacher was always frustrated with me. He made the assignments very clear—draw a bowl of fruit or a 3D box—but I always veered from the assigned work. I wanted to be creative, but I wanted to focus on food. I spent most of my art classes

secretly drawing dishes and dreaming of dinners I could create.

I used these drawings like diagrams, with each ingredient named and shaded in with color. Drawing became a new tool I could use for cooking, and it made me think more visually about what I was making. The most important aspect of food was still the taste, but I was starting to see the value in its presentation as well. The shapes and colors of ingredients became driving factors for new dishes. Could I make a dish entirely orange? Could I make a dish only out of foods cut into circles? What if everything on the plate was green? I found myself looking at plates of food like exquisite paintings; instead of paints and brushes, I was using sauces and spoons.

As it is for a painting, composition is important to how you experience a plate. In painting, composition centers on the way objects are arranged on the canvas and how that arrangement affects the viewer. The composition of a plate of food is equal parts vision and taste. The ingredients need to be arranged beautifully on the plate to satisfy your eyes, but they also need to be balanced to satisfy your palate. The correct proportions of each ingredient can only be determined by tasting the dish as a whole.

My plates became more artful as I began to develop my aesthetic style. I was inspired by delicate paintings with many colors and textures and wanted my food to emulate them. I was drawn to ingredients that matched these paintings. Interestingly shaped vegetables, flowers, herbs, and vibrant sauces became frequent components of my dishes.

This attention to visual detail was important in all the food I made and ate. When I prepared a simple lunch of deli meats and a salad, I would spend time trying to twist the meat into a flower, then realize that it looked ridiculous and change the whole thing until it looked right. I couldn't sit down and enjoy the meal until it was just so.

Even after I was satisfied with the composition of the food, I needed the right "canvas" for the creation. I would scour restaurant supply stores until I found the perfect plate. Once I found the perfect plate, I needed the perfect silverware. This went on and on until I had determined every aspect of the dining experience.

My love for details in the kitchen easily transitioned to the dining room. With each pop-up, I changed the space in some way to reflect the meal. In the fall, there were piles of leaves on the floor, which meant a lot of cleanup, and in the summer, fresh flowers and a plethora of fruits and vegetables adorned the tables. I wanted the space that guests were dining in to be as important as the food they were eating, so I spent as much time thinking about the setting as I did the food.

Every time I ate out at a restaurant, I would pay close attention to detail. How did the fork feel in my hand? How did the lighting affect the food? Was the chair comfortable enough? All these details were small, but if something felt off, I found I wasn't able to fully absorb the dining experience. A meal encompasses much more than just what's on your plate, and for me, what I put on the plate naturally led me to determine the rest of the experience.

My newfound interest in the experience outside the kitchen led me to a fascination with design. I didn't have much knowledge of design or of any designers, but I wanted to dive into the aesthetic world the same way I dove into cooking.

I started with research. I read books and spent hours on the internet looking up designers and design theories. I was mostly

interested in how design affects dining rooms and kitchens, so I focused on those areas. After a while, I found styles that resonated with me and that inspired me to make changes to both my kitchen and dining room. Similarly to when I started cooking, there were many obstacles, usually because I was in someone else's space and couldn't change their entire dining room just because of an idea I had. Through experimenting, I found ways to use the essence of these inspirational designs to make the spaces I was cooking in feel unique.

I often had to make items myself. If I wanted unique tableware, I had to either find it used or find new ways to use old tableware from my family. When I wanted spotlights so the food would be lit like artwork, I had to find a way to install lights on the ceiling without permanently changing the space.

The creative satisfaction I got from cooking easily transitioned into the design of the dining space, and then continued into every part of my career. I always searched for a blank canvas or a blank plate or an empty room so my imagination could run wild. In the course of exploring all these design interests, I found that the idea of finding your way through research, inspiration, experimentation and execution can be applied to any medium.

All I needed to open up my eyes to creativity was a spoon instead of a paintbrush. So what's your spoon?

this is not a
forest

This Is Not a Forest

Nature is the center of many art forms. The colors inspire paintings. The sounds inspire music. The flavors inspire food.

Growing up in California, my friends and I spent a lot of time running around in the fields by my house. One day we discovered some clover-like grass with yellow flowers that tasted like lemons when you bit into its crunchy leaves. Every time I saw it after that, growing in cracks in the street or on a hillside, I would stop to pick it. I never thought too much about this plant until a few years later, when I read about a restaurant called Noma in Denmark.

Noma foraged for most of its food. This meant they went into the woods in Denmark and found most of their ingredients in the wild. For a kid like me who loved exploring, this was the perfect combination of cooking and running around in the woods. Flipping through the pages of their cookbook, I found familiar ingredients, like the sour clover-like grass called wood sorrel, its lemony flavor coming from something called oxalic acid.

I started searching for wild food manuals to help me identify wild plants. It was thrilling to discover that food was around me at all times. I would walk through the woods or along the beach and think of dishes the same way I would while I was in a kitchen or grocery store.

When I went to the beach with friends, I'd snack on beach mustard, a spicy and vibrant-colored flower, or search for flat rocks that I could serve raw shrimp on. On a hike in the woods, I would look for pinecones to cook in syrup, or woodruff to make ice cream with. I couldn't walk down the street without seeing something edible or reminiscent of a dish in my mind.

I had become increasingly drawn to Scandinavia after learning about Noma. I continued to be inspired by these countries in my cooking and learned about other restaurants in the region. The nature-focused aesthetic of new Nordic restaurants provided much of my inspiration. Theirs was a new way of cooking that appealed to my California roots and detail-oriented personality.

The Danish word *hygge* is the best word to explain the Nordic style of cooking and hospitality. Hygge describes a feeling of comfortable friendliness and high-quality living that brings contentment.

hygge

(hyoo-guh)

I became so drawn to the style of these restaurants that I knew I had to go experience them. At age sixteen, I was about to finish high school, and I had saved money

from my job at a local restaurant. I had spent my entire time in high school pushing through my academic load so I could finish early and start to travel. My plan was to go to Norway and work for three months. My parents knew I intended to move after I finished high school, but Norway was farther than they expected me to go. Thankfully, my godfather was living in Denmark, so they felt comfortable letting me travel that far—and to a foreign country, no less.

I found a restaurant in Oslo called Maaemo that was willing to accept me and headed there shortly after graduation. It was my first time visiting Europe, and after years of studying the restaurant scene there through only cookbooks, I was exhilarated to be going in person.

I arrived at Maaemo for my first day filled with nerves and excitement. When I entered the kitchen, I was greeted by a familiar face: a cook I used to work with back home in the United States. He gave me a tour of the place and introduced me to the other cooks. They came from all over the world and were attracted to the same qualities of the restaurant that I was. Immediately, I noticed the care and attention that went into every detail. The food and interiors were beautiful and had a strong connection to nature. The dishes we made often looked as though they'd been scraped from a forest floor but had somehow exploded with elegant flavors and refinement. The service was warm and attentive, and the team worked together as one. At the end of my first day, I felt at home.

I was just an intern in the kitchen, so my tasks revolved around the many foraged garnishes on the plates. One of my daily responsibilities was to ride out to the forest with a couple of other interns and collect as many pounds of wood sorrel as I could for a dessert made from sorrel and shortbread. I'd hunch over for hours, collecting box upon box of the small, clover-shaped leaves in the wet Norwegian forest. When I found a damaged piece of sorrel, I would eat it as a snack and feel like I did when I was younger, sliding down hills and eating weeds. The only difference was that I was wearing a chef coat now.

My three months in Scandinavia changed my outlook on food. I found a new fondness for simplicity and an ever-deepening appreciation for nature. I also learned about a new way of life within my passion. I had spent all my time interested in cooking focused only on kitchens and the life that exists within them.

After my time in Norway, I realized I didn't have enough appreciation for what happens outside of the kitchen walls. The chefs I worked for showed me the importance of the connection between ingredients and the sustainability that comes from a balanced lifestyle. They were passionate about an all-encompassing idea of food, one that cares about the way the vegetables are grown, the way the animals are treated, and the well-being of the chefs who cook the food.

When I returned to the United States, I settled in New York City, where I had always dreamed of opening a restaurant. I had spent a lot of time there as a kid with my family, but after my travels, I looked at the city through a new lens. I strived to find the same pleasures in nature that I had discovered in Norway in the concrete jungle of Manhattan. I'd sit in parks and observe the pine trees and look for wood sorrel growing out of cracks in the street.

If I had never traveled, I wouldn't have discovered these perspectives on my craft. I continued to go far and near whenever I could and to learn as much as I could about other food and cultures through reading

and research. All these new perspectives helped to broaden what I appreciated in life and shaped what I wanted out of it.

Exploration comes in different forms. It can involve something as large as traveling to a different part of the world or as small as noticing your current surroundings. I was able to discover my initial draw to Scandinavia by reading about natural cooking. And even before I could go there, I found ways to explore my own version of it at home.

Whether you're in a Norwegian forest or your own backyard, there's always something new to discover.

this is not a
restaurant

This Is Not a Restaurant

Community is an essential part of any craft. Be it coworkers, family, or friends, having a network of people you can rely on can make a huge difference. Of course, creativity is a personal endeavor, but you need the help of others to see your vision through. In both good and bad times, coming together as one is what allows an idea to flourish.

Every day around four p.m., restaurant teams sit down together to eat what's commonly referred to as family meal. From executive chef to dishwasher, the entire team assembles over one meal that they cook for themselves. It's a time to appreciate the joy of cooking for each other before you cook for others. It's also a time for the team to bond outside of task-based work.

Restaurants are spaces that are always filled with a diverse mix of people from all over the world. Restaurants can act as sanctuaries for people escaping hardship or they can function like a school for young cooks looking to learn. Every day, the restaurant has a goal to achieve, and it takes every team member to make it happen.

Having diversity within a team is what makes a restaurant great. A good team can pool their collective knowledge in order to push the restaurant forward through creative thinking. On a rough night, they'll look out for each other and lift up even those at the lowest end of the hierarchy. A dinner service acts like a collective consciousness and brings the team together as a family.

I was always attracted to smaller, more familiar-feeling restaurants with diverse teams that worked together seamlessly. This was exactly the kind of restaurant I had always wanted to open.

After settling down in New York City and trying out different styles with my pop-ups, it was time for me to actively pursue my dream of owning a restaurant.

I knew opening a restaurant wasn't going to be easy. To open the place that existed only in my dreams, I first needed to find partners. I wanted partners who could help fund my concept and support me with the business side of things, but I also wanted them to believe in my artistic vision.

After I found partners willing to invest in my vision, I had to get to work on the space itself. It was finally my time to design every aspect of it. Throughout the process, I realized it was remarkably similar to creating a dish. I started with each room the same way I started with an ingredient for a dish. But rather than deciding between carrots or beets, I was choosing between stone and wood for the kitchen. I also found that my relationship to the craftspeople making the furniture, plates, and silverware very similar to my relationships with the farmers and purveyors. These same mental motions that I'd become comfortable with in creating dishes made designing a restaurant from scratch not seem so foreign.

Now that the space was ready, it was time to put together my team.

In order to have a successful team, I had the huge task of trying to make a new group of cooks and servers instantly feel like a family. I needed everyone to pull together like the great teams I had worked with before. In the past, I'd sometimes struggled to get older employees to respect me and my ideas. I was nineteen now and had learned that the only way to gain respect was to lead with mutual respect and to work with my team down to the smallest details.

I got rid of the traditional brigade structure I'd spent so long working within. I wanted everyone to have equal opportunities to learn and create. I wanted cooks to be able to talk to guests or learn a new skill from the waitstaff in the dining room, and servers to learn skills in the kitchen.

Anyone was welcome to come work at the restaurant. The only requirement was a passion and excitement for what they were creating. The team I brought together was full of people with different upbringings and backgrounds, a diverse crew with a united view of the restaurant.

I named the restaurant Gem, after my mom recommended that I spell her name, Meg, backward. It was an homage to the feeling of comfort and family from our dinners at home. When we finally opened the doors, I looked out onto a dining room that felt like a home and a team that felt like a family.

Years of hard work and determination allowed me to achieve my dream of opening a restaurant in New York City. But the dream grew into one of working together with a team that shared the same desire to better ourselves daily.

gem

mes

this is not

perfection

This Is Not Perfection

Creating something requires a lot of focus on goals and, ultimately, on perfection. Even in this book, I've included a lot of stories and examples of looking for perfection, of trying to achieve something grand. But while striving toward perfection is natural, it's essential to remember that it's only part of the process.

It will come as no surprise that I categorize myself as a perfectionist. I've spent far too many hours redoing things and stressing until things reached "perfection." Even in the process of writing this book, I've gotten stuck on sections for days, trying to think of the perfect thing to write.

Having gone through this process for over a decade now, I can begin to look at the things that I once obsessed over and see the downside that comes with seeking perfection. This is something that was very hard for me to grasp. I would beat myself up over the smallest detail, which created a lot of anxiety and stress around a passion that had initially brought me joy and calm.

When I opened Gem, I struggled a lot with this balance. Cooking always brought

me to a peaceful place, but now it was heavily weighed down by employees, guests, and expectations. About a year in, after months of worrying about unachievable napkin folds and being disappointed about awards we didn't immediately receive, I started to feel overwhelmed. At the time, I was reading a lot about a Belgian interior designer named Axel Vervoordt, and about something called wabi-sabi.

Wabi-sabi is a Japanese philosophy that appreciates the beauty in imperfection and transience. In design, it means finding beauty in the imperfection created by nature. In the philosophical sense, it's about finding the joy in the impermanence of life through fleeting, imperfect moments. I felt it had a lot of similarities to the Nordic cooking I had been so inspired by.

侘寂

wabi-sabi
(wah-bee sah-bee)

As I started to look for beauty in natural imperfection, I found my style of food changing, as well as my attitude toward it. When apples would come in misshapen, I wouldn't spend all day stressing over cutting them into cubes. Instead, I found a way to showcase their natural shape. I stopped writing specific recipes and instead encouraged the cooks to rely on their intuition. Not every fish that comes in is the same size, so why cook them for the same amount of time? I continued to simplify my dishes and found that I was able to go to sleep without fixating on the smallest mistake from the day.

I started to slow down and appreciate the small moments of my day and the art that comes from basic tasks. Instead of thinking far into the future, I was finding more joy in the act of doing everyday tasks without a more specific goal in mind. I still had goals and dreams to drive me, but rather than fixating on them, I focused on the tangible joy I got from my passion.

I don't think I would have gotten to this point if I hadn't strived for perfection in the first place. If I'd never pushed for perfection, I doubt I would have ever been able to see the beauty in imperfection. It may sound confusing and make you wonder why I would recommend thinking in two opposite ways. It has all been a part of my creative process, I guess. When I learned to find the beauty in imperfection, I learned to respect the process itself, not just the goal.

For a long time, I had focused on opening a restaurant. Now that I'd achieved that goal, I realized either I needed a new one, or I needed to recognize how much creativity goes into living your passion every day. This switch helped sustain my creativity instead of burning it out.

I got to these places through reflection. As I wrote this book, I had to consider how my creative process has changed throughout the years. I used to think reflecting on things before you reached your goal was a waste of time. But as I thought about my early creative process, I realized that most of what I was doing was constant reflection. I'd make a dish and reflect on it to learn how to make it better; every night I'd reflect on the service to see what I would change. My process of refinement came through reflection.

Reflecting, refining, and allowing your opinions to change is how you continue to create endless possibilities. The creative process is filled with reinvention: even after you reach the goal you've set for yourself, there will continue to be endless things to create.

The journey of self-discovery and creativity is a never-ending road, so enjoy the ride.

Recipes

These are some of my favorite recipes. They are for everyone to eat, but not for everyone to make alone at home—I make them in my restaurant. Although a young person can certainly follow them, some of the equipment needed might not be readily available, and in some cases it would be best for an adult to be present. Whether you execute these recipes or not, I believe reading the ingredients and instructions will help encourage creative thinking, inside the kitchen and out. It's good mental exercise to find recipes you think you'd like to try. Cooking is a process of experimentation, and the discovery is part of the journey.

Beet Wellington

(Serves 6–8)

This recipe is the culmination of many years of testing. It has turned even the biggest beet haters into beet fans. It is definitely the most complicated recipe in this book, but if you take your time, it will work perfectly. Picture a Beef Wellington, with crisp pastry wrapped around tender meat. Now swap in beets, savory mushrooms, and a rich, deeply flavorful sauce.

FOR THE WELLINGTON FILLING:

BEETS

INGREDIENTS:

1 lb red beets, peeled and quartered

5 large beets (any variety), roughly 5" in diameter, peeled

1/2 cup (1 stick) butter

Salt to taste

Preheat the oven to 250° F. Turn on your smoker and smoke the quartered red beets for 20 minutes. Juice the beets by first blending them until smooth, then straining. Place the 5 large beets in a baking dish and cover with the juice; add the butter and salt. Bake for approximately 4 hours, until the beets are soft. Strain the juice and continue to bake the beets in the oven until they shrink a bit, then set them aside.

MUSHROOM DUXELLES (A FANCY TERM FOR MINCED MUSHROOMS)

INGREDIENTS:

2-1/4 lbs cremini mushrooms, finely chopped

1 tbsp and 1 tsp butter, separated

1-1/2 tsp soy sauce

Heat a large sauté pan over high heat. Add the tablespoon of butter and let it come to a foam. Add the mushrooms and soy sauce. Cook over medium heat for 10 to 15 minutes or until tender. Strain the mixture through a chinois (or any fine mesh strainer) and reserve the mushrooms on paper towels to dry.

TO ASSEMBLE THE WELLINGTON:

INGREDIENTS:

40 blanched red Swiss chard leaves, stems removed

10 sheets puff pastry, cold (storebought frozen pastry is fine; thaw in the refrigerator the night before), 12" x 12"

Mushroom duxelles (see recipe above)

Dried beets (see recipe above)

To blanch the greens, submerge them in salted boiling water until they turn bright green. Pull them out of the water with tongs and place them in a bowl full of ice and water, to stop the cooking process. Strain and squeeze out any remaining liquid.

Place the puff pastry on a very lightly floured flat surface. Lay half of the greens on the puff pastry first, to cover a 5-inch area. Spread a very thin layer of duxelles on top of the greens. Place the beets in the middle. Cover the beet in mushrooms and then wrap the whole thing in the remaining greens. Wrap tightly in the puff pastry and trim off excess. Reserve in the refrigerator.

FOR THE TOPPING:

BORDELAISE SAUCE

INGREDIENTS:

4 beets, cut in half and charred under the broiler

2 yellow onions, cut in half and charred under the broiler

3-1/4 cups sliced smoked beets

3 tsp butter

1/4 cup diced carrot

1-1/4 cups sliced shallot

3 tsp tomato paste

2 tbsp red wine vinegar

2 tbsp soy sauce

2 tbsp honey

To make the charred beet stock: Combine the charred beets and onions in a large pot with 1 quart plus 1/4 cup of water. Bring to a boil, lower heat and simmer for 30 minutes, then drain.

Sauté the sliced smoked beets, carrots, and shallots in a pot with the butter over medium heat until the vegetables take on a deeply caramelized color. Add the tomato paste and cook for another 2 to 3 minutes. Add the red wine vinegar to deglaze the pan, using a wooden spoon to scrape up the browned bits at the bottom. Add the honey and soy sauce. Add the charred beet stock and cook down the liquid until about half of it has evaporated, or reduced. Season with salt to taste.

SMOKED DATES

INGREDIENTS:

6–8 dates (1 per person)

1/4 cup applewood chips

Heat the wood chips in a pan until they start smoking. Add the dates, but keep them far away from the wood chips. Cover with foil and smoke for 5 minutes.

TO FINISH: Combine the components into a layered Beet Wellington pastry.

INGREDIENTS:

1 egg beaten with 1 tbsp water

3 tbsp heavy cream

1 cup red Swiss chard chiffonade

Lemon juice to taste

Salt to taste

Bordelaise sauce

Smoked dates

Preheat oven to 350° F. Brush the finished pastry with the egg mixture and bake on a buttered sheet pan for 20 minutes or until golden brown. In a small pot, heat the cream until it boils. Add the Swiss chard and cook for 10 minutes or until most of the cream has reduced and glazed the greens. Season with lemon juice and salt. Slice the Wellington in half and season with finishing salt. Add a mound of your creamed greens, a spoonful of the Bordelaise sauce, and a smoked date.

Roast Chicken with Bread

(Serves 6–8)

We make this at the restaurant every Saturday for family meal. It's a perfect easy dinner, and the bread soaks the juices up nicely. You can change the vegetables to anything that you have available.

INGREDIENTS:

1 medium-sized chicken

1 loaf sourdough bread, cut in half lengthwise

3 leeks, sliced into 1/2" rounds

2 heads fennel, sliced very thin

2 shallots, cut in half

8 carrots, cut into 1" pieces

1 head celery root, cut into 1" cubes

1 head garlic, cut in half

12 sprigs thyme

Salt and pepper to taste

Olive oil (for drizzling)

Leave the chicken uncovered in the fridge overnight. This will help dry out the skin and make it extra crispy. Preheat your oven to 385° F. Place the two bread halves facedown in a roasting pan. Scatter the leeks, fennel, shallots, carrots, celery root, and garlic around the sides of the bread. Place the chicken on top. Season liberally with salt and pepper and drizzle olive oil over the whole thing. Add your thyme and lemons and place in the oven and bake for 20 minutes per pound, or until the chicken is golden brown. Let the chicken rest for 20 minutes. Carve the bird and serve with the vegetables and bread.

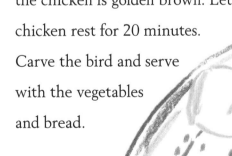

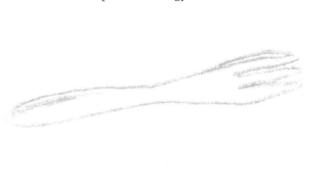

Mushrooms with Creamy Polenta and Ricotta Salata

(Serves 4)

A great side dish that is also a base you can add to. Use it to explore different kinds of mushrooms.

POLENTA

INGREDIENTS:

3 cups whole milk

3 cups water

1 cup polenta

1/4 cup crème fraîche

4 tbsp unsalted butter

Kosher salt to taste

Bring milk and water to a boil over medium-high heat in a medium saucepan. Reduce heat to medium. Gradually add polenta, whisking constantly; bring to a simmer. Reduce heat to low, cover pan, and cook 30 to 35 minutes, whisking continuously, until thickened and soft. Remove from heat and add crème fraîche, butter, and salt. Whisk thoroughly.

MUSHROOMS

INGREDIENTS:

1/2 lb hen of the woods mushrooms

1/2 lb shiitake mushrooms

4 tbsp butter

2 tbsp minced shallots

3 tbsp sliced chives

2 tbsp white miso

Juice of one lemon

Salt to taste

Cut the stems off the mushrooms and clean off dirt with a pastry brush. Heat the butter in a saucepan over medium heat until it foams. Add the shallots and cook lightly until they start to barely turn golden around the edges. Add the mushrooms and the salt. Let the mixture cook for a few minutes before you stir it; this will help the mushrooms release moisture and caramelize better. Cook the mixture for 10 to 15 minutes until mushrooms are soft, stirring every few minutes. Stir in the miso, chives, and lemon juice.

TO FINISH

INGREDIENTS:

2 oz (about 1/4 cup grated) ricotta salata

Spoon the polenta into bowls and top with the mushroom mixture. Grate some ricotta salata over the top to cover the dish, and enjoy.

Fried Cod Cakes with Tomato Saffron Sauce

(Serves 6–8)

This was one of my first "aha" recipes. I offered it on almost every menu I made from ages thirteen to fifteen. It's a take on a classic brandade—a sauce combining salt cod, potatoes, and olive oil. When I wanted to make a brandade, I couldn't find salt cod, so I ended up making it with regular cod. I like how fresh it tastes.

COD CAKES

INGREDIENTS:

2 heads garlic

1 cup extra virgin olive oil

1-1/2 pounds Yukon Gold or any thin-skinned yellow potato, peeled and diced

Salt to taste

1 cup whole milk

10 sprigs fresh thyme

1/2 lb cod

2 tbsp lemon zest

1 cup flour

2 large eggs, whisked

2 cups panko

2 cups grapeseed oil or other neutral oil, for frying

Preheat oven to 325° F.

Make your garlic confit (garlic that has been slowly cooked in oil or any fat): Place the garlic heads and olive oil in a small heatproof dish and cover with foil. Cook in the hot oven for 1 hour or until soft. Remove from the oven and let cool. After the garlic has cooled, peel it and add it back into the oil. Discard the garlic peels.

Bring a pot of salted water to a boil and cook the potatoes until soft. In a wide skillet, heat the milk and thyme over a gentle flame until barely simmering. Poach the cod in the milk with a big pinch of salt, keeping the heat low, until the fish is opaque. Add the cod, potatoes, and garlic confit to a food processor with the lemon zest and process until smooth. Add the milk and continue processing until the mixture is a firm paste, like the texture of hummus. Spread onto a large sheetpan so the mixture is 1" thick. Freeze for a few hours or until firm. Once the mixture is frozen, cut it into squares. Dip the cod squares first in the flour, then in the eggs, and finally in the panko. In a deep, wide pot (such as a Dutch oven), heat the oil to 350° F (test with a fry oil thermometer) and fry the squares until golden brown.

TOMATO SAFFRON SAUCE

INGREDIENTS:

1/4 cup olive oil

3 cloves garlic, crushed

2 cups cherry tomatoes, halved

1 pinch saffron

4 tbsp warm water

1/2 cup bread pieces, torn

Salt to taste

Heat the olive oil in a medium pot. Add crushed garlic and tomatoes and fry for 1 to 2 minutes. Add the saffron to the warm water in a separate container and let the mixture steep on the kitchen counter for 5 minutes, like a cup of tea. Add the bread and steeped saffron water to the tomatoes and reduce the heat to a simmer. Add salt to taste. Cook for 20 minutes and combine in a blender until smooth.

TO FINISH

INGREDIENTS:

1 cup arugula

Lemon juice to taste

Salt to taste

Dress the arugula in lemon juice and salt. Place the fried cod cake on a plate. Top with the tomato sauce and garnish with the arugula.

Chicken Stock

One of the first thing I ever learned to make was chicken stock. It is *the* culinary basic and can be used in so many ways. My chicken stock recipe is based on one I learned in restaurants, with a few added flavors.

INGREDIENTS:

5 lbs chicken necks and backs

1 lb chicken feet (optional)

4 quarts (16 cups) cold water

8 cups ice cubes

2 onions, cut in half and charred under the broiler

2 leeks, cut in half, cleaned, and charred under the broiler

One 3" piece of ginger, charred under the broiler

2 carrots, cut into 1/2" rounds

3 bay leaves

10 sprigs thyme

20 black peppercorns

6 dried shiitake mushrooms

Rinse the chicken parts and place them in a large stock pot with the water. Bring to a simmer. Skim off the impurities that rise to the top (I use a ladle or a spoon). Once the liquid is simmering, add the vegetables and herbs. Simmer the stock for an hour or longer, depending on how rich you want your stock to be. Strain the stock, then quickly dip the bowl it's in into a large pot full of ice water, also known as an ice bath. This will stop the cooking process.

ACKNOWLEDGMENTS

This book couldn't exist without Beverly Horowitz guiding and pushing me the whole way. Thanks to everyone at Delacorte Press and Random House for excitedly making this happen, and to Adil Dara for understanding my aesthetic vision better than I do.

ABOUT THE AUTHOR

Flynn McGarry is an American chef based in New York City.

This Is Not a Cookbook is his debut work for young people.

ABOUT THE ILLUSTRATOR

Adil Dara is a designer and artist based in a tennis club in the California desert.